Ode To A Toad

By Dan Bryant

First published in the UK in 2021 by Stour Valley Publishing

A CIP Catalogue Record of this book is available from the British Library

ISBN: 978-1-913450-67-0 (PB)

Printed & Bound by Mixam UK Ltd, Watford, UK for:

Stour Valley Publishing
N4 Blois Meadow Business Centre
Blois Road
Steeple Bumpstead, Haverhill
Suffolk
CB9 7BN
www.stourvalleypublishing.co.uk

For Sally

Ode to a toad

Dry skin bark-like, awful bumpy,
Mouth suggesting he is grumpy.
Happy hiding in the dark,
With golden eyes that shine and spark.
A clump of soil that struts about?
Independent, short, and stout.
Confident and self assured
The toad shall always be adored.

Smooth newt

How cool, how slick, how in control.
How smooth, this newt, how rock'n'roll.
He braves the rain with no umbrella.
He really is a stylish fella.
In and out of cool fresh waters,
Newt's about, lock up yer daughters!

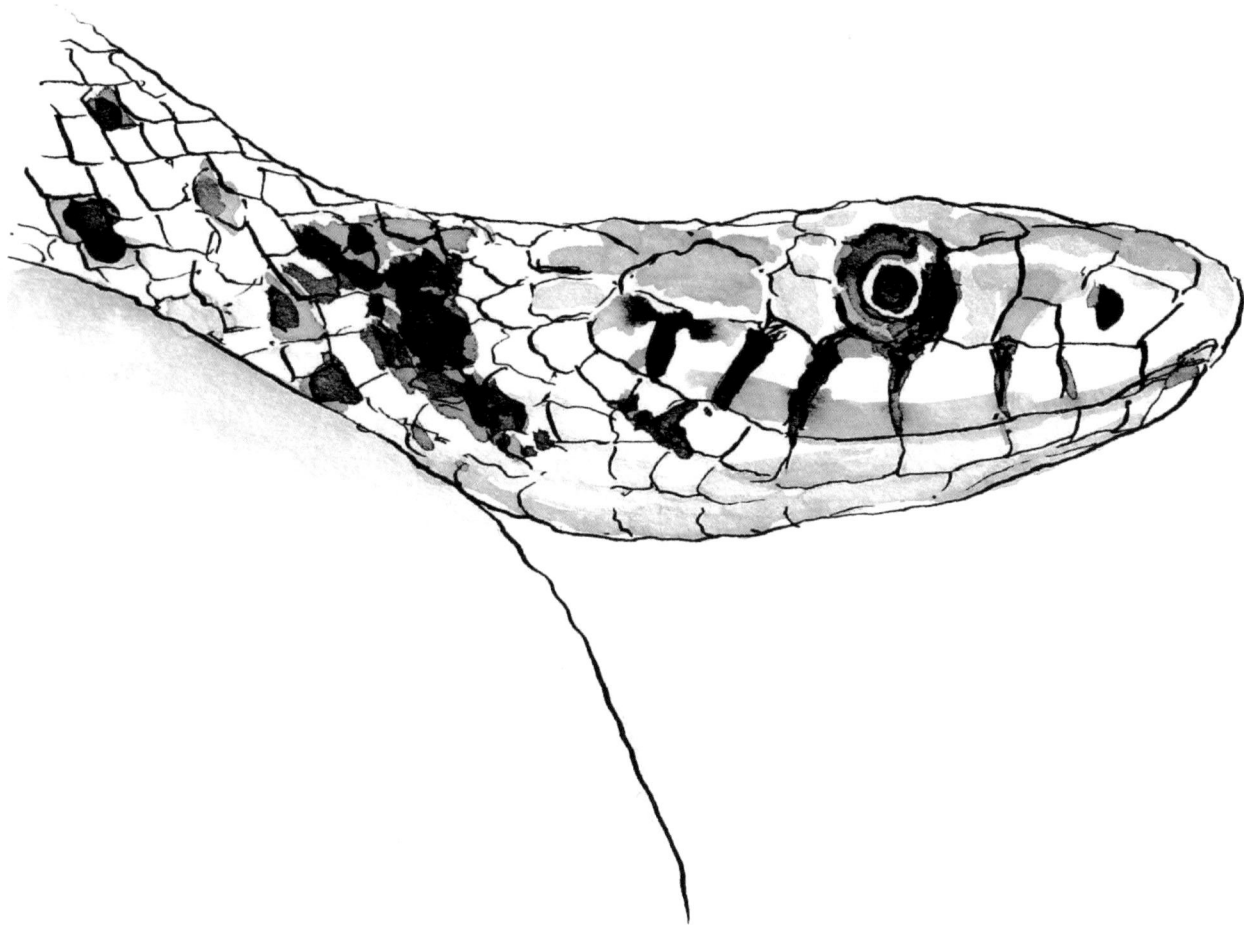

GRASS SNAKE

Contentment is personified
When grass snake takes a swim.
A pond or stream or in a lake
The water's fine for him.
His food is frogs and ducklings.
He swims with grace and class.
With all this talk of water,
What's it got to do with grass?

Slow worm

Slow worm, slow worm,
Where d'ya want to go worm?
Sunbathe? Find shade?
Show yourself or hide away?
Slow worm, slow worm,
What d'ya want to eat worm?
Chomp slugs, munch worms...
Does that make you a cannibal?
Oh! Worm's a different animal.

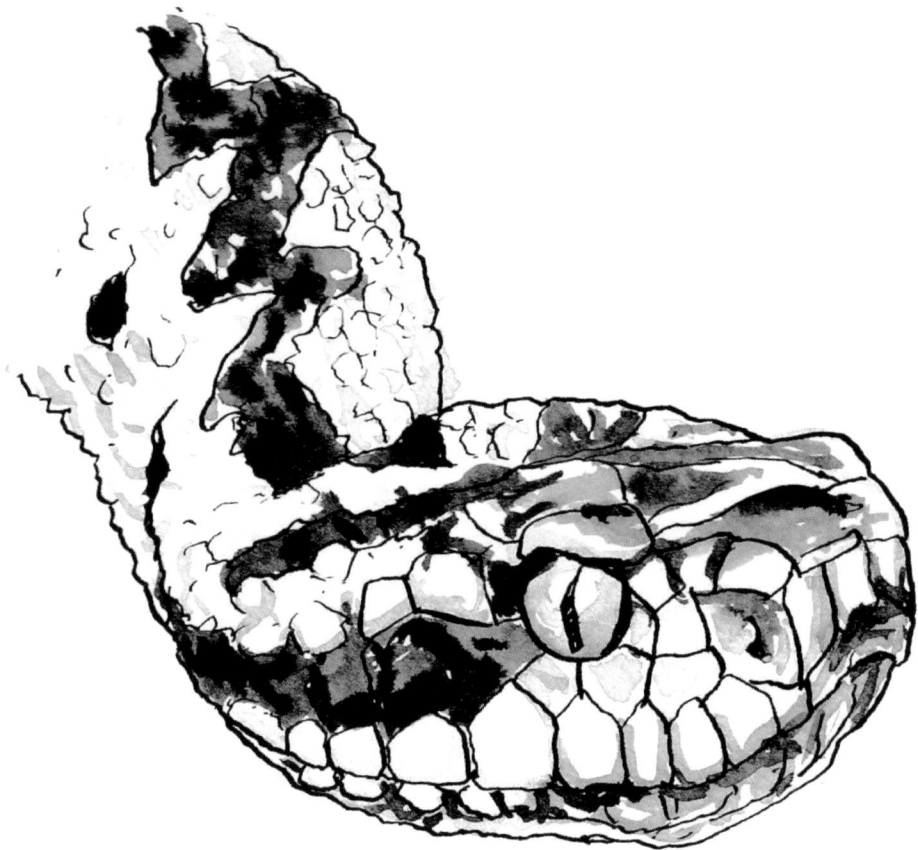

The Adder

A serpent of beguiling charm,
The adder is respected.
She never means us any harm,
When venom is injected.
So use your eyes and mind your feet
When you pass by her house,
She may mistake your little toe,
For a shrew, a vole, or mouse!

Great Crested Newt

The great crested newt,
So majestic in spring,
Like a miniature dragon,
Such a glorious thing.
He dons his best outfit,
And dances his dance,
And kisses the lady newts,
Given the chance.
He never gives up,
Like a true Casanova,
He remains 'on the pull',
Till the season is over.

Common frog

Exuding a slime that defies all description,
The shy common frog hides away with conviction.
Coiled like a spring, with his eyes open wide,
His pupils dilated, and off to the side,
Spying a threat and unable to stop it,
He presses them shut and takes off like a rocket!

The Natterjack

A clever toad, the natterjack,
To stop cars parking on his back,
Paints yellow lines all down his spine,
The cars are towed and promptly fined!

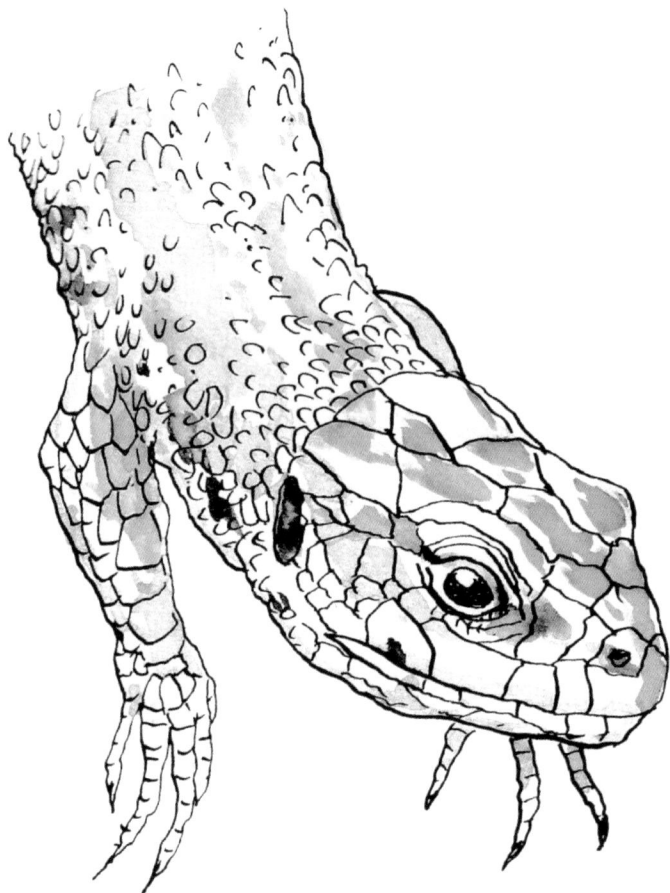

THE COMMON LIZARD?

What title shall this lizard choose,
Viviparous or common?
The latter one does not amuse,
The former one too modern.
Then after many sleepless nights,
And many grunts and groans,
The little chap has changed his mind,
To either 'Smith' or 'Jones'.

WASP

Black and yellow, black and yellow,
Never means to hurt a fellow,
Yellow stripes on stripes of black,
Stinging point found at the back.
The wasp, so often whacked and swotted,
When, at picnics they are spotted,
Really should be left alone,
To taste the jam atop your scone.

Woodlouse

The woodlouse, as I'm sure you know,
Dwells in the damp and dark,
She loves to hide in rotten wood and under bits of bark.
With seven pairs of tiny legs she scuttles
When she walks,
She pays no mind to gossip as she rarely ever talks.
She whiles away the daylight hours nibbling away,
At all the damp decaying wood that underneath she stays.

Dragonfly

Garnished with bedazzling jewels,
Emerald and sapphire.
Big and bold, and beautiful,
This dragon breathes no fire.
They swoop around the garden pond,
Like little fighter jets.
What if they really can breathe fire
but haven't found out yet?
Perhaps one day a dragonfly,
while zooming past my head,
Will blast out flames...   well, to be safe
I'm going to stay in bed.

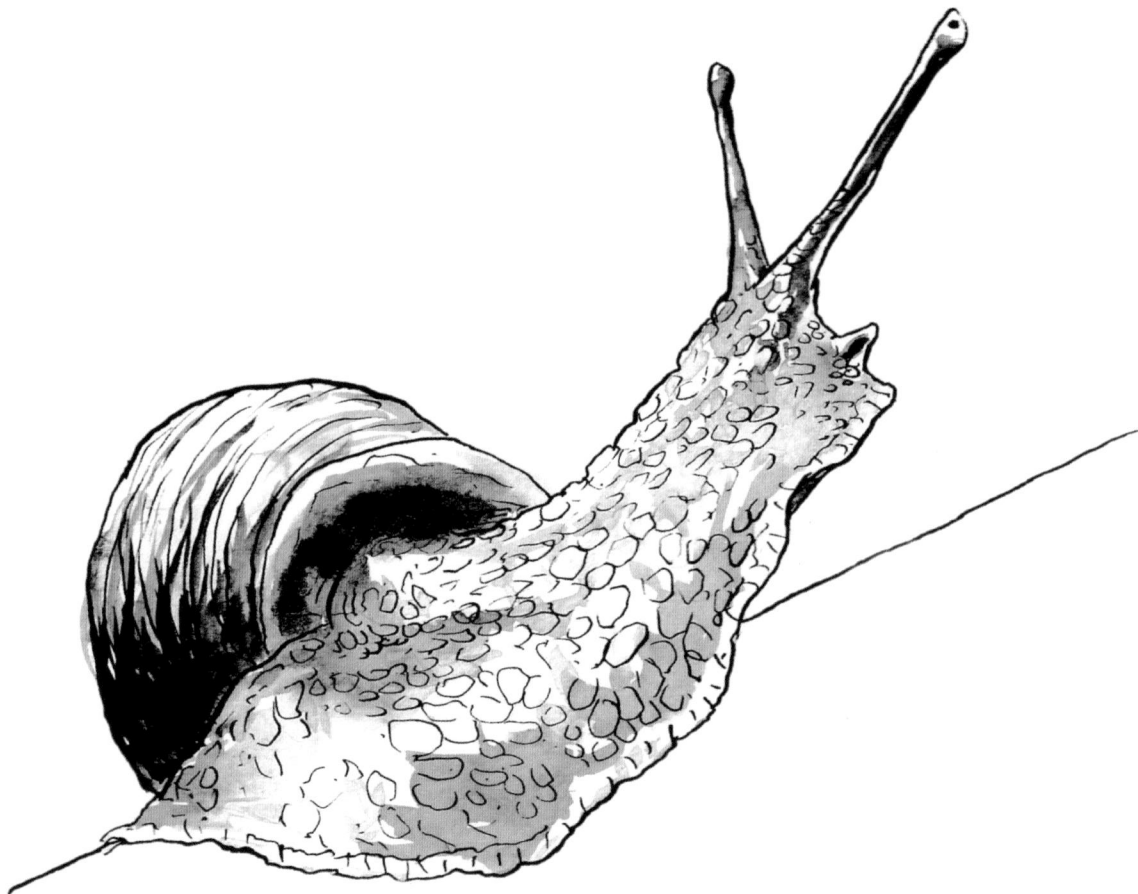

Snail

Happy in the rain,
Eyes on stalks.
Only ever crawls,
Never walks.
Hiding in a shell,
Free to roam.
So jealous of the snail
and his mobile home.

Sand lizard

"Oh sand lizard, sand lizard
Where do you stand lizard
Where is the best?
Well, where would you rest?"
The lizard replies,
A glint in her eyes,
"I choose to reside,
To no one's surprise,
Right here where I stand,
Right here in the sand!"

DAN BRYANT

Dan Bryant is an author and artist living and working in beautiful Exmoor. His passion for local wildlife - in particular creatures that slither and crawl - has grown over the years since first drawing tadpoles in his 'topic-book' at first school.

Email: danbryantart@gmail.com
Insta: @danbryantauthor

Here's something you might like to know...

We print and distribute from the UK

Our printers only use environmentally certified and recycled papers

All papers are from sustainable sources

We insist on the use of superior quality vegetable based inks

Both we and our printers recycle all waste products.

SVP
STOUR VALLEY
PUBLISHING